Julie —
Thank you
for everything.

— Critt —

*For my sisters: Anne and Emily*
*and my daughter, Kaya Hope*

# Looking for Small Animals

*Caitlin Grace McDonnell*

LOOKING FOR SMALL ANIMALS

Published by Nauset Press

nausetpress.com

New York

Cover and Book Design: Nauset Press.
Cover image: *Fantastic Ornaments*, L'Aventurine, 2007
ISBN 978-0-9851268-7-2

Some form of these poems have appeared in the following journals or websites:
"Pomegranates Turn Upward"; "Instructions"; "Ghazal" in *apocryphaltext*
"In Defense of Gathering" in *Boog Lit*
"Answer"; "Stichomancy" in *Big Bridge #12*
"Sumac" in *Cacohophony*
"Morning" in *CHRONOGRAM*, November 2005
"The Dealer" in *Insurance*
"Dreaming the Tree"; "Karma"; "Dogs"; "Form and Content" in *La Petite Zine*
"Sleeping with Emily Dickinson" in *Louisville Review*
"The Dealer "in *The Hat*, Winter/Spring 2000
"Walking in Provincetown" in *Shankpainter* 43

A chapbook entitled *Dreaming The Tree* containing some of these poems
was published by Belladonna Books in 2003.

*"Ah, who can we prevail upon to use in our need? Not angels,
not humans, and the resourceful animals already note we're not very at
home in the interpreted world..."*
–Rainer Maria Rilke, "The First Elegy"


*"'It's a little Anxious,' he said to himself, 'to be a
Very Small Animal Entirely Surrounded by Water...'"*
–A.A. Milne, "Winnie the Pooh"

# Contents

## Dreaming the Tree

Not the tree, but the lake
dreaming the tree, shimmering
this brisk meeting.

Tracing the private finger
along the alphabet of other
upstairs, alone, breathing...

Brushing off the imprint
where light didn't hit
what accidental beauty.

The trees are receptive;
*we're all ears, they tell me, start with*
*the father and fall from there.*

How'd I get this wild?

Oh, money, father,
sister, lover on the other side
of walls, you who brave

the tiniest selection—what
falls away? What gathers?
*You have a gift,*

she said from underground.
Unearthed, he had just straw,
stones, a blue comb.

*Keep this,* he said, turning away
in his floating chair. *Hold on,*
*listen, what else—*

I

## In Defense of Gathering

It can happen anywhere;
the unnamed thing comes forth,
and claims its place
at that long table of the ordinary.
The poet is someone who listens,
who hears voices, an eavesdropper.
Orpheus was postmodern before his time,
a gatherer, not a hoarder, of the whispers of
the dead. Eurydice was the true poet;
she was talking in her sleep, didn't know
she knew until she said it. Words
jetting out like blood, up through the thin skin
of the earth, her Vesuvian face smiling
as still as a window.

When you look up and see the sign:
*Blind Children Passing,*
or even: *Keep Your Valuables Close to Your Person,*
or in the Hollywood movie, when the man
speaks intimately, horribly, to his date:
*I envy your beauty, I want it all to myself,*
at the bottom of my spine, I feel a new
guest pulling out his chair, grinning
in black jeans. Doesn't matter
that he's late. He nods politely at
the other tired truths, says:
*The name's Suspicion,*
*I'm the reason she never trusted you.*

## Pomegranates Turn Upward

Conformity is right for you. Ask
your advisor, only a minute walk
from neveragainland. A sharp,
potentially uncontrollable increase
in threat. This is modernism in both
thought and action.
Who is going to take care
of you. Maybe he's protecting a world
he loves from a world he hasn't had time
to mend. Nothing is more valuable than
leaving a good history behind.
No such luck. Life is totally about losing
everything. It's always perilous
to predict the end.
For instance—pomegranate flowers,
oversized and blood red, turn upward.
Manuscripts in bookstores, libraries,
countless watercolors in her studio
on the second floor. I suppose it was
a strange childhood, but it defined
their lives. The wound feels like a great
inflamed jewel glowing in the dark.
I did not accuse a single angel.
Without psychosexual drama or getting fucked,
she might just grow
a beard. He waits for more, but there is no more.
A warm, steamy rain comes next.

## Emotional Intelligence

In the dream, Anne introduced me,
*This is my sister Caitlin,*
*she doesn't always do what's good for her.*
I felt like she was leaving me then,
in the way one does, shrugging:
*there are limits to this give and take.*
I never imagined knowledge
as a free floating mass of words,
clicked on, saved on a chip, but something green
or dark red, running through stems, up
through roots and veins.
If there's any kind of afterlife,
I figure it's in the touch:
your father's father in your collar
bone, this coin still warm when it
reaches my palm, I finger the grooves
of want, spend it, breathing:
this is instinct, this is money,
I learned the difference.
It's in my shoulders. Touch them.
Win a lineage of lovers in one bed.
Sit down at 23rd Street on a bench,
pull out a notebook and write:
Fear used to lead me around on a leash—
Now there's nothing left to be afraid of.
No such thing as a bad dream,
just dark corners to avoid,
and this relentless rainy task:
transliteration of green.

## Night

I dream I am raking the father
perfectly—
Japanese sandbox of ashes;
two male friends at my side.

Beside me, my lover dreams
of sex with a man.

*Dreams are just the psyche
trying on its wardrobe*, he says.

All night blue, glistening angels—
Gabriel in his silk dress—
dance over our floating bed.

## Feral Ghazal

Lichen thrives in adverse environments, mountaintops and ice.
A feral animal is one that has escaped domestication.
St. Augustine's definition of God was a being whose center is
everywhere, borders nowhere.
The process by which any technology disembodies us is called
angelization.*
In a basement in California, a woman sleeps cradling a phone.
The heightening of one sense necessitates diminution of the others.
All change begins with disruption.
The process of one animal taming another is both violent and loving.
And you, Caitlin, what will it take to hold you still,
pockets filled with sea-swept stones.

* This line is from "Angelization" by Nick Flynn.

## Monarch

Watching them promise
To have and to hold
one another up over
gravity's intentions,
I grip my words, tiny
jagged stones, gemmed
in my tightening palms.

Leonardo called the arch
the force originated by two
weaknesses. After the wedding,
the preacher leaves a wing
on the plate between us.

And later, another elegant
moth—not collectable, but
common—offered her part-
dead struggle. I tried to take it
by one side, but my desire
shuddered her to flight.

The dust of somatic decay,
the body relinquishing
to soil, stained my fingers as
they recoiled back to fists—

like that immortal man
of marble, chipped down
to his one bright question.

## Telos

1.
History must have an end;
sign of a larger death, skin, music, oil, breath—
achieving its ultimate purpose.

The death of art,
the taste of summer sweat
need to be understood to a further—

to a further.
She can't lift her head.
She, so attractive
because she's so tired,
not at all to a higher mode of existence,
which requires the otherness of matter,
beautiful.

It's sweetly humid behind her knee,
what Plato calls the shadow world of space and time.

She coughs violently,
spits some of last night's dream—
women with shaved heads,
into the white room.

2.
Thought kills what has life.
Black leather gets hot in the naked sun.
We all have these feelings
I have disclaimed.
We are unraveling.
A black shoe, left somewhere in the woods in the dark;
mere appearance—a gentle drip
of cool catharsis in two poles.
Sunlight on a sheer white skirt.
We create history to explain the immediate.
Hegel says, *To try to give myself solace*
*by withdrawing*
(she touches her neck)
*is to live in a fantasy world.*
We run our fingers through our hair for Hegel.

## Realism

I did imagine violence, in the halflight,
the nude shimmers; in this stark bright,
an ass folds over the dirty sheets, remains an ass.

For months she has been trying to write
about sentimentality in postmodern literature.
I gather she is against it.

Her poems are interesting coins in my hands;
I used to read them again and again,
looking for some opening I could crawl into.

The place where I love her is enormous,
bruising, luminous, unreclinable; pulls
me up from the back of my ears.

I see the glass animals lining the interior
of your chest, in strict rows of sobriety
standing firmly four-legged and staring out.

Haul the poison seeds out the back of your throat,
I want to pull this up from below the dirt.

## The Moth

The animal started lashing
at fifteen. Who am I kidding.
Vermouth and apple juice. I lost all
my friends but two. As it should be.
I love to bare him. Love to love the male
form, not just when it bends me
over. How easy he's ready; the clown

in the box, the catch of the wind
on wings. This month is about finding a place
to sit. About who to sit by. There's a scent

of algae underground and something
rising in this place in my chest.
There is always just enough.

And that's not even close to enough.
The animal paces in its cage,
roars, grows weary and glares.
I was born into the generation

that expects it all—
and we don't even know what it is.
We just know it can be bought

and blown to shreds in seconds.
We laugh at families on television
fixing things, staying in
their little yellow homes.

The people I meet mostly seem to want
something else, which they temper with travel
or pills. Some people do it anyway,
despite the absurdity, which I find beautiful.

They build a shack, get a couple of goats
and spawn. I've been trying
to own up to my life before it's over.

There's this sense of everything
piling and a moth at the window, knocking,
killing itself for what it sees and can't have.

## The Presocratics

1.
*There was a philosopher*, he said,
*who spent his whole life trying to prove*
*anything existed outside his imagination.*

*The shudder of a bird's flight overhead,*
*he says, without the bird itself...*

I had wanted to write about organs; how they
cut him open and replaced

the lungs, thinking: I wanted to be a woman,
wanted to be reached inside intentionally;
feel life grow out the lower rooms.

He likes to reach inside with the hand—
*The other organs*, he says, *have minds of their own.*

Mr. Johnson kicks a stone
and it hurts. The intersection is the point of entry.

When I wake up to a scream outside,
what soothes me: *Dogs bark*, Heraclitus says,
*at people they don't know.*

2.
Before the word,
when he turned his small back
the way he held *cunt* in his mouth,

months before I would mark his absence by
a rigged boat, before
the way time began to whip me.

When I see something for a moment
between genders, is it intellect
that pleases me? You weren't even there
at the words' birth,

It was a sea of text
you fell into, singing *Summertime*,
stumbling. *But cloudy, cloud is the stuff of stones.*

## Sleeping with Emily Dickinson

I would sneak in through the window,
bring her sweet meat.
We would giggle in white
nightgowns about the books,
laboring over her dashes,
her intentionality,
the skepticism of unrequited love.
I would be very quiet.
I would not say
what doesn't matter.
Take her to the window,
open it: tiny chimes.
Let down her hair.
Tease her about her attitude,
night-breeze billowing the
white curtains. Angel bellies. We'd share
a cigarette. She'd like that—
the slight slip of suicide
punctuating the moment.
Whisper:
>  *Where is it I go—*
*When we are Here yet both Alone*

Hold her ghostwhite Hand

whisper:

*I hear what you Don't write down.*

## On Being an Angel

*(after Francesca Woodman)*

He's a selfish lover.
Glass eye that takes
and takes. I'm putting on
hats, body black
and white, dusted out
of dreams.

Outside the barn, color.
She waits to take me
to the river. Autumn:
vibrant deathflakes.
Buzzard's breath,
the scent of snow,
something green
pokes out. She'll hold
my head in her lap,
soothe the leaping
silver. But in here—

he's got me fixed
in his mirror,
whispering:

*Stay as you are,*

skin translucent in his light.
*Come to the window,*
*final frame to hold you*

*still, perfect.*

## Thorazine

The unconscious has not a solid constitution;
it is liquid and it is air. Raining over sleep,
on a frozen dry field, gate left open, tired wood
screeching on hinges. Desolate but for a sole,
shock-white cow. Seeps through the blood,
mixing with anything orange,
shooting out through shoulder blades, fingers,
settling in the small ocean of the lower belly.
There are centuries of fathers wadded up in muscles
and a tiny breath breeze skittering leaves
along the streets of my breached birth.

You wanted to return me to a place I've never been to.
You wanted the bed to be just the bed,
the lock on the corner window
to eradicate the wind outside, the whole world.

*Taom* is a word that didn't survive translation,
it was too fast to catch, too big to fit through the cords.
You let it rest on your tongue like a planet.

Once harnessed, travel will always be deliberate,
any bed is a boat. The pane of glass was once flowing,
you remember, and you can feel the wind
slap your momentary skin.

## *Prayer for Sleep*

*There is no fire*
*in this house*
I lit them carefully
and blew
them out one
by one until
the dark came
and rode with
me and now
I long
to give
myself over
to that
under place
where stories
tell the truth
in funny ways
and nobody
real is
home.

## The Paraclete

*You need to slow down*, he said,
interceding his Scotch, tight
lipped in its little glass.

*Oh new religion, holy withdrawal
from life*, this body's insistent;
gasping, tied to this firm chair.

A chair is what the human
form is not; he's offering
peanuts, nude in their

papery shells. I shed
my rings, finger the flesh,
each digit a scepter of light.

You came with permission,
whatever the rapt
procession claims, eyes

fixed on my belt, the
ludicrous mane of hair—
and I happily traded

the score, not the sister
gifted the larynx spinning
its thin song, but the girl

on the shore is mine, corpse
washed and salted, clean
in her white dress, palms

cupped in the shape
of a question.

## The Mice

I must have heard them nibbling
through my dream—
like some nightchild
conjured in a cookie jar.

My parents' marriage
was small animals
hidden in cupboards,
among papers stuffed in drawers,
in the food.

Neither of us remembers
counting, but we both keep saying six.

They were fast gray babies.

On the roof, they disappear too quick
for my comfort, they're gone before
the scream has emptied, the city
just beginning to honk
and stutter itself awake.

Back in her room, wind crackling
the white paper
that lines her windows:
*You made that happen,* she says. *You mention a mouse
and suddenly there are seven in my kitchen.*

I am rarely really asleep. I'd wake as a child
from dreams of the house burning down
to find my parents screaming,
blind as mice in a can.

For me, the tiny sounds are deeply audible.

## Blue Mountain

Night in a purple cup.
The house becomes a field.
Stiff family of
chairs thinking in the
bright dark.
Wild boars in your dream
nudging the fence.
Invisible thread—
lay yourself down.
Let it tell you a story.
What are you made of?
Water, salt, memory.
Narrative stored in
each brave breath.
A blind man I know
said he could feel whether
a woman was beautiful
by the air around her.
There are many ways
of dying, these flowers
on my desk crimson
beyond themselves, they
can't help but flaunt
their peak too far
and bow down.
Old men weeping,
barely holding
one another up.
Sometimes I think
I've already lived harder
than these bones set out for.

Enough for the night,
hold the arrow down
on sleep, green light
left winking as I pull

thick blankets over
the world in
its narrow bed.

## Fish

What's so great about joy—
pain tingles too. Why
not rest in something
that might stick.
The world's big and
ruthless. I want to be small.
I want the time before the touch
when the air is folding
in lavender light. Before
the bed, before the knife...
Before the needle or the
string, the picture of the girl—
the moon conspiring with
the curve, the crook,
the mouth, her mind, her
time ahead of time stolen
and held still. What is happy
if not the tiny red the cat
will chase and never catch.
I don't want to be smart.
I want to watch a fish
in blue water with a plastic
mermaid, a castle; watch it
feel the fake pink plants
tickle the gold coins
of its belly and think
for a spell that the bowl
is the whole world.

## As Of Now

You must never say the same thing twice.
You must walk your longings on tip-toe
rather than tucking them in sleeping bags
with flashlights. You must learn waiting.

You must say *but if*, instead of *at least*.
You must learn listening. Not just to
small animals tucked in crevices
in cupboards and bodies.

But to strange, misguided arrows
that climb you mountains rather
than glowing lazily in still ponds.
All night genius will throw you

candy flowers. You must catch them.
You must fold each one, promising.

# II

## Letter to a Teacher

*for William Matthews*

At your funeral, I kept thinking: this is a grief I don't know yet.

A man who died without aging,
holding his pain
politely, in his apartment.

This country hasn't grown up like that.

We have grand provisions to ward it off–
a bus full of children dead;
someone wasn't doing his job...

(Our reader starts to lose his bearings here.)

At 24, you wrote: *There was a real lost child.*
*I don't want to swaddle it*
*in metaphor.*

The money won from my uncle's body
crushed between a wheel and metal;
compensation funded my education.

(And here you'd tell me to give more information.
We're not mind readers, and we're probably more
ignorant than you fear we might be.)

And no, you wouldn't suggest
I come right out and say it,
but the father needs at least to
make an appearance before
he's responsible for these
vague and damning implications.

Of course you weren't going to tell me how,
would shake your head in agreement:
my father's grief at his brother's death
was another poem.

*Sometimes you have to let it go, even when it's good, even when*
*it's better than the poem you're really trying to write.*

You knew poetry wasn't where the work was,
but the relief, the loose utterances
of the poet's real work,

which is mostly silent,

and more often than not constipated.

*The word poet is like the word angel...*

(You looked sad when you were being ironic,

having digested the limitations of connections, other minds,

how we store information and come home to our silent cats.)

*and angels don't do anything, they just hover there.*

*Verve, verve,* I'd repeat to myself after reading your comments,
You didn't separate my mind from my face

because that would be wrong, to pretend seduction
wasn't part of the process

of attaining truth, tangled in a golden mesh.

*That's why we call it art and not circumstantial evidence,*
you might deliver like the tragic stand-up,
and something about why we love music, and how much
closer it comes to saying it, what we can't, we can't–

*I don't know how to make you understand*
*that punctuation is emotional...*

(You knew that would spark something;
they're poets, you'd think, and in their twenties;
appeal to their narcissism.) The comma,
like a dip in the ground, a curve
of the spine.

Most of what you spoke hung in the air,
the three dots blinking
after it: *anyone, anyone...*

## *Walking in Provincetown*

Pull over and let your
tender one lead.

Sunset relentlessly passing,
press a stone in the palm,

its gift at commitment.
The story of your life,

all gesture, lapping
the shore, retreating.

Your insistence on living
tempers me like punctuation,

the tick of the clock. Even beauty
needs a place to hang her cloak.

I've never seen it all. Blues her,
reds me, a piece of sky

falls beyond the text—
its firm horizon.

The moon has tired
of earring metaphors.

She turns in her sleep,
reveals her better side,

as the sea answers yes,
anything you ask her:

*Yes*, should I stay, *yes*.
Should I go, *yes*.

Leaving you is shelling
a mollusk—its wet reminder

nude in the salt air.
Like Protestants, you want a road,

a map. *I Was Here* tracks the sand.
You were here and here

is where you lost something.
Where the beach arched

its back toward your mind
and you dropped the shell

you'd held like a child's ear,
tenderly, like it could lead somewhere.

## The Face of Joseph Cornell

He looks startled—no,
not startled, a kind of terror
at the time it took that wicked
eyelight, grain, emulsion;
the tiny home that would
hold him still.
I've seen him before.
I think he lived in our basement
growing up. He was the child
of the hippie woman who cried
and quietly brewed things below
our long, abstract dinner table.
They left in a sweep, forgetting
a green crystal beneath
the fading yellow chair.
My sister and I passed it
back and forth between
our pink fists, piece
of the precious underworld,
fetish of other families.
We kept it secret, promised to hate
all future tenants,
having found our currency.
He knew the boat would be there,
parallel to the triangle
of his green kerchief, folded
cautiously in his right
pocket. He knew it would sail
to the periphery of his outer
vision, waves rippling
in direct causal relation
to the map of his brow.

## The Lake House

Everything seemed small,
our adult bodies fumbling
around the dreamtiny kitchen,
distance to the one red store.
The house had been preserved
like a museum, as if even moving a book
would eradicate the smell of pine, the aura
of Papa filling the freezers underground
with ice cream bars he convinced us
the house produced on its own accord.

I believed him, never having
known something with history.
The strong arms of the stone
fireplace holding up the ceiling,
wood with its swirls of eyes,
Orange aureole glow of the lantern.
yellow quilt, rough grasses of the carpet
that skinned my infant knees and
the couch in the living room with
a shadow around it of something

taken. The hollowed cry of the loon.
The lake, still as a mirror. At the grave,
my sisters and I lay our bodies out and felt
the unearthed ground. A sudden white horse
appeared; his limbs tight, outrageously twitching—
yet he stayed still enough to let me reach my hand
through the flies' incessant buzz
and place it on his jowl.

## Form and Content

This poem has an anonymous woman in it.

It is going to make you watch the birds peck out her eyes.

It will so convince you of the grief of the world,
you will actually enjoy the way the birds eat at the woman.

Somewhere there is a boy
searching through aisles.
His hunger is all he knows.
It gnaws at him like urban dogs.

That terrible surfacing we keep thinking against.
Like fear, it makes the ears feel hot,
the chest a vacant wind.
The little mouths of it eat and eat.

The hunger is the woman.

The hunger is the birds.

The radiance is a fourteen-year-old girl.

She sees straight through salt lust bone meat—
and she is free
in her horse body,
free of longing.
Free of longing for longing.

*Take, took, taken*

Her face
becomes our use for her face.

## Hybrids

Let's live in this illusion,
we've been traveling a long time.

In photographs, as children,
we look wild and suspicious.
Me—still and confrontational by the Volvo,
shovel deep in the dirt.
Your little muscles tightly defined,
by climbing and climbing,
quixotic, determined.

Your lover is married,
but you're far away from that on the farm.
You spread a hand-
woven Guatemalan
blanket over the truth,

and cross-breed seeds
in the soil outside the
wooden house you're living in
for now, built by the man down the road,
in the Ozarks, in middle America.
As the century attempts
to name itself, to lay itself down,
you're springing up Primaxes,
Safekeepers, Burpees' Sureheads—
vegetables our parents never heard of.

## How to Say Segue

This is about the real world,
which happens in hospitals,
kitchens and cars. God isn't around.
Steve talked a shitstorm before he died,
or so I'm told. I was running around
New York City with whiplash,
mostly underground, coming up
for nimble meetings and juice.
I didn't get there 'til he was a thin slip
gasping digitally through tubes,
dark green thoughts thrumming
loud in the white room, leaving
us to carve them with language.
He put out a bowl of phrases.
Mine was: *Take care of her*,
which worked for me. I folded,
pocketed it and scurried out.
Death's a whale's head nudging
the boat, father's eye, drunk
and spinning, hand you drop,
let fall in its puke.

The waiting room was
a strange orgy, all of us piling
on stiff chairs, neat stack of
magazines to leaf through
maniacally; Julia Roberts,
happy as a clock. TV locked
in the upper left corner,
jerking off. Which reminds me.
San Francisco University Hospital,
third day, the music changes and
the surreal walks in on its tall fins.
She decides to bottle his sperm.
This isn't fiction. Suddenly we're
all red-faced and laughing on
linoleum floors. *I was worried
at first*, Doctor Stulberg proclaimed,
triumphant, *but then I hit gold.*
*He'd be so happy to hear that*,
someone giggled. Pale, scarred
body spurting its last hurrah.
It was like we all came with him,
temporary relief, slight shame—
we lit up, exhausted, having briefly

conquered death. Clay took his time
driving from Denver, but when
he spoke,
it was loud and clear:
*This isn't a Fucking High School Reunion
for Chrissake, my Brother is Dying.*

When life leaves, it's subtle;
pond dries, screen fades
to white; body slips
into a new pronoun.
In the end, I played the catcher
in the hallway. Amani was standing
one minute, diagonal the next.
Immediately after he'd finished
sobbing in my hands he hated me
for holding it and that was fine.

*Segue*, he told me at the funeral,
beer spiny with fruit at noon,
paper plates swollen with
hummus and corn. Everyone milling
like Noel Coward on Xanax.
*For months before he died,*
*he kept saying seeg,*
*and then I seeged into this, he'd say,*
*or then it seeged into this other thing—*
*That was my first thought leaving*
*the hospital after it was over:*
*Segue, goddamn it; it's segue.*

## Karma

*Be careful what you ask for*
a long haired boy used to tell me.

His father used to invite him
to watch porn flicks. He lost

interest as soon as I said yes.
There's what you're dealt

and how you play it. He died stubborn,
smoking in a floral chair, enough anecdotes

to savor another 40 years, cats
licking the dry white bowl. Had his

father's heart, like these dimples
my Mother passed down as currency

or armor. *People pay for what they do.*
Baldwin said, pillars of debt, our solitude

arching before us like those
varicose roads we're lost on.

*and they pay simply.*
Pull off at the Red Hook Diner,

*by the lives they lead.*
Take down your hair.

Look for a clean shaven
Samson, clean fork, weak

coffee. Order an omelet.
Ask a stranger to point.

## Early Motherhood Divorce Poem

Congress of empty chairs, of damp leaves on dark streets,
assets transferred of whatsoever and when, dividends, loose ends.
Dips in the ground where sticks pulled up bits of earth    pauses, full stops,
     bearings, curses, cursors,    the jujitsu of terror.    Define dependence
the names of your children.    Fill in the blanks    pull in the reins
The rain shrugs and lifts itself up    press the dry ingredients
between fingers and rub them with butter.    Gently express the excess
milk down the drain.    Leave a space for former spouses.
     I hate feeling hatred. A nursing child will not look to us searching and
fearless inventory    like a horrid man smoking a cigar.    You want it to be tender,
but still have a tiny bit of crunch. In a well-nourished woman,
     rebuilding of maternal reserves begins    The petals unfolded on their own
timetable before    breastfeeding ends.    with sunlight and water.
Individual, joint, totten trust, treasury notes. Shifting
between    these roles necessarily raises questions. What the child wants and
needs are no longer the same.
     The books long to be drained of their letters,    pipes churn around
this wave of white sleep. Her head smells of dirty snow.
     Adjust as necessary.

## Sumac

I know everything. I think about this when I'm outside your doorway, leaning my bicycle against a tree, impatient to be inside, knowing we'll argue and unfold, that anything could happen. I have two places where I am always in bloom; the rest is potential. I cannot read and love you simultaneously. You can tell your dreams to a lover or you can write them down. I wore rosewater in six countries and was always two places. I walked on white limestone cliffs in Kusadasi and breathed in your shoulders. You held my hand in the dark, in the woods, and cried because you could not let me love you. I can sustain myself, and I think about this when I, not bleeding, haven't cried that I can remember, smell the sweat on my shirt, ride by the limitless scent of aloneness. Both of your eyes, in two places that are everywhere, remind me of a small animal that lives in my stomach. The room I am in is lined with different colored squares with directions: This switch is for that computer, or: Put your scrap paper in the garbage. I need to drink water or smell your skin. He held me too long against his skin on the porch and cried and let his tears sink into my own. It gave birth to a smaller, darker animal. I can't see its eyes because it rides on my back. Its hands touch my shoulders, but I am on a cliff, where if I yell as loud as I can, if both animals, both sets of small dark eyes yell with me, it will echo. Sumac makes a pretty good tea. You can hold it in your hand, in the dark, in a big empty barn in the woods, let the red beads crumble and moisten your skin. There are two places to go and you have to start somewhere. You can consume it. You can steep it and drink it with hot water. It will drip down in your stomach, fall on the eyes of the small animal living there. She had a recurring dream about a cow in an open, snowy field with a gate around her that was open. When they walked in the woods, he showed her the beast he sees when he goes there alone. I heard it running beside me, as I ran in the dark, toward the sumac. I don't remember the scent, but at night, the red beads and my sweat and aloneness all smell the same. I lean my bicycle against the tree, and as I let go of it, I'm deeply saddened, in these eyes, in my stomach, and my shoulders ache with the small dark grip because I know that the door has weight too.

## Narrative

The body says:
*Lie down, taste this,*

*want what's easy.*

The slight movement in water
that circles out...

The world heals.

Wild thyme grows elegantly
over a grave, forgetting.

The mind says: *Fight to take me
with you.*

Sitting on this gray tray, spiced
and steaming,

in want of caress.

They meet in a white room.

Everything's real clean. A lot of waiting.

A book is lying open by the window,
which is also open.

And the book is waiting too,
doesn't know what for—

fat with its glum story.

The wind exhales in with a new mouth,

      shuffling the pages

## Stichomancy

*Let me say this,* he said at one point,
*I'm not sure if I can solve the problem.*
*Now, go back to the gift shop*
*and get a knife from the drawer.*
*Make yourself comfortable.*
His foot moved from brake
to accelerator to brake.
Between us, a relationship
was always going to be a mistake.
He had always arranged his life
so as to protect himself
from the shock of disappointment.
This is probably supposed to tell us
something about the artistic endeavor.
The narrative voice jumps
between the characters—
so vulnerable and earthbound,
neatly bearded, subdued,
slightly blurry, untouched
by either sentiment or irony.
He exudes power, but is not comfortable
in his own flesh.
The world is a dogfight.
He would become the master.
She is unworthy of even as base
a miscreant, a woman blessed
with keen intelligence
and generosity of spirit.
This is no longer the case.
He thought of his apartment,
of taking off his shoes at the door,
as he always did. He thought
he should do something other than drive.
She did not keep a very neat kitchen,
but he tried not to notice.
Several weeks had passed, and that
was a humbling experience.
Where does she say, *Oops,*
*I got it completely wrong?* Even
an ardent feminist found herself
identifying totally with the dry witted
heroine. She does manage to be funny.
She did not bring any extra provisions.
The effect is part *Alice in Wonderland,*

part Eurydice. The long-term risks
of this path are well known. The works
look demure and pastoral from afar; up close
they pack a heavy political punch. The
unconscious selfishness that cuts people off
even from those they are closest to. We're
here for life. There's a paradox I've never been
able to work out. What I don't believe in, I suppose,
is certainty. The angels are kind, like waiters. I think
it's the kind of issue where something looked extremely
difficult and not worth it, and then people changed their minds.

## Get Smart

1.
The woman was holding her sweater in her teeth,
slipping in the disc that brings the glow
of words. She's sexual, I noted,
yet not possibly like I am,
or those I've closed that
wide door with, gnawing at one
another, like creatures you
don't see in ordinary light.

2.
I spent three hours in a bookstore
in Berkeley, leafing through
Dylan Thoma's dedication,
breakdown, divorce, something I'd felt
exactly; it had to be personal.
Or maybe I was looking for flesh,
some opening I could crawl in,
curl my mind around those verbs:
*to be, to be...*
It's as if I thought the typeface
would emit a smell or touch me back.
The clerks were starting to stare;
I thought I was looking for poetry,
but wound up with a hot
pink book with a blurb,
the most sexually explicit novel
ever written by a man.

3.
This morning on the six train
you pointed out agent 99,
who was aging very well.
*She wore great clothes as an Avenger,*
you recalled. *It was a very cool part.*
I think of you between my legs—silk,
lavender and peppermint over my eyes,
as I breathe in all your effort.
The golden dog with his ears perched
at this peculiar sound, peers at our
entanglement, how can you sit
so still and stoic next to me,
as we creak through this metal vein
under all those buildings,
cement, choreography. Coming,

I forgot everything I knew,
everything I count on you
to know, just peppermint,
lavender, a red hyacinth
bursting in my throat.

## Ghazal

The night's an ink spill and my womb's an envelope.
Drive around and around yourself in a red car.

Never trust a man who can always get it up.
The clock insists and the trees lean in like aunts.

Red wine costs me 3 dollars and 33 cents.
That man and I, we got on like a house on fire.

Across town, he sits and regards a deep blue screen.
Happy are those who have what they once longed for.

The child upstairs declares his bright existence.
The scent of meat wafts through the dark backyards.

And you, Caitlin, whom do you ask to find who you are
as this night winds around you like a sorry train.

# Oz

Horse of a different color;
fields of dizzying flowers
leave me weak kneed
in my blue dress. And you,
a little man with a megaphone.
In Kansas, you shone—
in the papers, on TV. *The bigger
the bark*, Aunt Em snapped,
sippin' Scotch, *the smaller the
curtain rope.* Your stock
of hearts, it's said, is low.
The scarecrow's a breeze;
seven years propped on a stick,
blackbirds burrowing his brow,
yellow straw steeped in their beaks.
And the cat with the mane can't
hear his own roar. But my shiny man
of metal, my armor, mi amour; he's
a reconstituted Chrysler,
a Cadillac incarnate. I found him
hacking his ax in the tall woods,
tin legs and arms stacked up
like shrapnel, mumbling thinly
about a munchkin girl in Emerald
and wanting to be a better man.
I slapped him together with what
remained. An axle shaft,
a hatchback latch—He hooked
my itinerant elbow in his left lever
and we eased on down, fueled with
promise and petrol. I told myself
it was just the occasional jump-start
he needed, not the lack of a ticker entire.
But somewhere between Liberal and
Gillikin, he began to sputter and stall.
Finally froze in a way no oilcan will
quench. Tin finger on rewind, gaze
fixed on a familiar screen. Well now,
Precious, me and the dog walked one
brick too far down this jaundiced joint.
Click of the sequined heels. I'm for damn
sure there's nothing in that black bag for me.

## The Dealer

*Life is a deck of cards,*
said the voice on the phone,
*and this is the hand you've been dealt.*
She was talking to my mother,
voice firm as the grip
on the back of a cat's neck.
I'd found her crouched,
head in her hands, papers,
bills, forms, strewn over
every inch of the floor.
*Leave, honey,* she'd
managed, low and guttural,
like the dying engine of the silver
Volvo in the driveway, which I dreamt
of finding stuffed beyond capacity.
He had filled it with our things:
clothing, books, furniture, dolls
with their insomniac gaze flattening
against the window. No point of entry;
the car as much a mockery
of its origin as the objects inside.
Somehow, she got up and out of there.
Her hands, which had always given
away her age, held a hidden flush,
a full house or two pair.
She now sits in another home,
with space and sparse decor, a view
of the little city and a light she plugs
in at winter to emulate the sun.
The muscle of her heart as tough
as vinyl. Me, I'm still in that driveway,
turning the key, my foot pumping
the pedals, replaying the revving
of the ancient engine, recording
the burst of the radio, singing *1969.*

## Answer

The bottom, the true bottom of grief
has no name. It is what happens before

the wind and its subsequent motion.
The stream that runs directly from

your soul brings blank white windows.
Still, you bark the question again

and again in the night's crevice.
Meanwhile, words like *caution*

bump around you in the dark.
There is what you do and what you

spin out of the gold thread that patches
together the flimsy dream. The tiny

red wired envelope. And you were
mighty thirsty, weren't you. You bent

what you could, and when you got to the place
where the car drove on its own accord,

and the skin sealed around itself, you
lay down in the dirt and froze. You

wanted to serve. You wanted to empty
your organs and stroke their flatness

like old plums. You wanted the world
to finally read you, and yet on the top

of the hill, there were ants, weeds.

## Youth In Asia

I was driving Persephone when I got the call
She'd been walking in circles around her bowl.
(Summer school in California, we'd named the cars
after Greek gods.)
*You better take this one,* Aram told
me, tossing me the keys,
*It seems to be becoming your car.*

It took three days for the vet to start using
the word. I'd nod slowly with sleep deprivation,
picturing children, rows of desks across the world.

*It'll be over by the time I take the needle out,* he
proclaimed and left. She stilled.
White cloud. Immovable Tongue.

All other griefs surfacing in the silence.
Abortion: arbiter of life and death,
medical hand pulling the curtain.
Amani and I talked about Stephen
at San Francisco General five years

prior; something familiar
about the light. Afterwards,
I smoked on cement steps
by a mural of Gandhi's face.
I had to pick up the four students
who had chosen a Ferlinghetti reading

over a bonfire. *I say we go to Berkeley,
pick up Ferlinghetti,* Amani suggested,
*take him to the bonfire, throw Paloma
on the fire while he does the reading there...*

I laughed and looked out at Highway 1,
its edgy thrill still novel after ten years
in New England's woods. Insistent waves
crashing against cliffs. Across the globe—
a young boy writes in ink at a window
tenderly stroking each word.

## Instructions

It is time to drown the girl.
The one folded  into a passport in your pocket,    sewn
in your blue dress, legs flung open like a forked road
            as she rides your shoulders.
Remember the shoreline and pay your respects.
Know that if you allowed your torso
            to be drummed absentmindedly
in a dorm room, in the 80's, California
morning, it is still yours listen to the tinny music
            beneath the skin.
Use every currency while it's at your disposal
but keep the door        to your room full of bees
            sealed with a gold stamp.
Remember how you grew a body
by looking at the backs of eyelids and only show the ones
            who make it to Eldorado
the society of chairs
            made of clean, red stones.
Remember the view from above. If you find yourself in Athens,
            full moon, having climbed the acropolis,
confronted with a fenced-in barking dog,
            remember what the monk said
regarding the center of things—
            how you're always at it.
The small, seemingly misguided
voices of authority you find in dreams    desire heeding.
            Generally, you know. Whenever the question is go
or don't go, jump or don't jump,
            the answer is easy. When the question's manifold,
            savor the discomfort, it's just the tireless
and always hopeful ivy of your mind seeking other planets.
It is time to lay down your scrolls. To open your mouth
and clear your jaw of its pursed mantra.
            Time to let yourself forget. The way a child learns
to read by remembering a voice on the edge of a bed
            and its relation to the    great green room of the page.
The way you say *amour*  and name another history
than love and the way a  body learns another body
            carves it like soap        in the shape of a C, facing inward.
Others will regard you as a clean pond they'll see past
            your soliloquy straight into their own selves thirsting.
They may miss the girl. Have compassion,
Be patient, grant        visitation.

## The Blue Raincoat

You left somewhere in the night.
Rain and the hard chemical facts made me
stay. I woke to his pale skin, touch like a father's,
a question mark, muscles poised between comfort and sex.
When I kissed his ear, it was angry, a clear little stone bargain,

A debt without perimeters,
leaned back on his bony form,
waiting religiously for light. I knew
we weren't going to name it, but I made him
let me wash the dishes, stacking white bowl against bowl.

I walked down the cobblestone stairs
with him at my back like a curtain. Outside,
young people sat on the grass, the stretch between
river and sea. I didn't know why it was called Spanish
or Arch, or restaurant. I am the age he was then. In dreams,

you are outside windows
carrying garbage. They're behind
the cash register telling me not to wave.
You'd just stand there, not knowing when to stop
waving back. I can't write about this any other way.

Memory teases us,
hovers at the top of the stairs
we fall down, faithfully describing
the step we're on, its dusty stone surface.
The expanse toward the bright crack of the doorway,
dark face fading at the back of our skulls.

## Midsummer

I play the ingenue,
mince my rage, don't eat
meat. Talk about wives,
divert my eyes. Lately,
all we do is dip in
and out of the blue
pool. Liquor burning
our throats, steam
of flies with permits to
bite: red cloud
mirroring out.

She night-strolls,
barefoot in white.
Dreaming, led
by a moon's
cool drift.
Mosquitoes gossiping; their
long needles threading,
yellow grasses wet
beneath her.

This is how we write our lives.
Away from them.
In a vain hotel, weak
coffee, drapes drawn
over the screen's loud
math, all our plans
and promises stored
on a train, her
whistle's shriek drowned
in the dark heat,
creak of her effort,
a strong heart
listening, leaving town.

## Silver Stallion

*O please, Mr Policeman, I'm lost in the wood.*
Between the lightning and the thunder.
*soft soft soft hand.* I am lonely here now.
Oh, touch me soon, now. Use of placebos
would not lower costs, since a predetermined
number of participants approached the sacrament.
Failure to answer as required shall be deemed
an admission of liability. Knows the taste
of them now. Old Father Ocean. That one
is going too. Privileges suspended. You express
a great deal of anxiety over our willingness to break laws.
A cloud covered the sun, slowly, wholly, shadowing
the bay in a deeper green. The answer lies in the fact
that there are two types of laws. What did I say?
I forget. A conscientious proofreader attempted
to mend it at the surface. *And what is death,*
he asked. *Your mother's or yours or my own.*
This response is not justified by the information
in the excerpt. Other interactions across cultures
can serve to disseminate ideas and discoveries.
Hat square on head. Buckles shined and cleaned.
Young shouts of moneyed voices. The discovery
spread to the Arab world as a result of warfare.
Phantasmal mirth, folded away: muskperfumed.
The detection of temperature by a finger touching
a cool surface. I remember only ideas and sensations.
The spread of papermaking technology, increase
in breathing rate while exercising. In my mind's
darkness a sloth of the underworld, power's blank
voice spoke. This relationship is not linear.
*As I am. As I am. All or not at all.*

## Everything

The snow came down like an afterthought.
Like elegant wallpaper, a pilgrim dress,
a simple shake of the head. Total lack
of emotional involvement can change
your nights. I have a problem with
boundaries, and these activities have
tempered this instinct for forgiveness.
He took a step, and another, and went
on, amazed, focusing on trees growing
wildly in fields. He stayed quiet and
hydrated, kept flashlight use to a
minimum, but was later observed
making all too human errors. No points
will be awarded for guessing what happens
next. Like many great adventures, this one
begins with a passageway. A maker
of fences in the nineteenth century
advertised a new kind of fence as being
"bull strong, horse high and pig tight."
Blackberry and wild rose and unnamed
vines entangled so thickly as to make
a wall. People tell you to use your brain,
to use your body, and those are well
and good. I snatched up a length
of two by four and began to tear
at the earth as if I'd been born to it.
It doesn't take much of a nudge
for the subtext to rise to the surface.
He acted on his instinct to cure
his fears by plunging into them.
She stands there clad only in a pair
of black underpants, but this too,
is wrong. It makes her sound sweet,
whereas she is actually tough and wise.
As usual, the region, a "sensitive area,"
is being evacuated. Through the tree,
she made out the almost inaudible sound
of breathing. The said sun, an enormous
orange ball, peeks through. "All right,"
he said, "if it is that important to you,
it is everything." She absent-mindedly
rubbed her thumb across the glass,
cleaning off a fine layer of dust.

## Resurrection

1.
Pissed-off inward, proclaimed the nurse,
and pressing: *Does this hurt?*

I think: *Lady, I don't know what pain is.*
*What hurts you?*

It feels worse than eating oatmeal,
Better than a donkey stepping on your foot.
Better than a nail driven through the palm.

*Fear of change*, my friend tells me,
and I figure we do store up,
hold our own
bodies of water
in fear of lack, reverence to drought.

2.
At eight years old I stood twelve feet
above ground on parallel bars
and closed my legs.
The Dungeon Drop, having a name,
seemed harmless,
landed me on my right arm,
like a wing, enfolded.

All through the service,
I'd stare at my palms.
How could a nail drive through
bones, blood, but
I'd feel the heated place it happened.

*Caitlin isn't here anymore,*
I'd sing, eyes ghost-widened,
blank as bleached dolls';
she begged me to stop.
My throat tickled
as I pressed on:
*Does this hurt?*

3.
You suggested I write about being somebody else,
but while I know how to step out
of this frame,
I question the potential
to truly inhabit.

I can reach my hand in you
and recognize that internal—
like the palm's hollow cradling.

I used to think the most we could say
is: *I'm like you.*

This morning I think resurrection
is just what happens when we're in pain.

And maybe it's really: *I see you.*

## Slipstream

The towers fall. A baby wakes,
but she isn't a baby. She's just small,
and no longer occupies your insides.
Meanwhile, there's a line around the block
for the store with the glowing apple.
Or is it a hotel? It's not a call to arms.
We're trying to reduce the damage.
In the article about integration, the white
child is named Prairie. She is the only one
in focus. *Some people are light,* your daughter
says, and *some are dark. You are spotted.*
Meanwhile, the little city of your childhood
is aflame. The elementary school is accepting
small animals. There are men putting
rubber fingers in your mouth and prying
it open with tools. They ask you questions
as if to taunt your speechlessness. This, too,
you will endure. Turn off the glow of the screen.
Nobody owns anybody. You've reached
your quota for aphorisms. Lay down
each vertebrae and let the steam roll
up from beneath the earth and take you
down to the dream of the gate, the house
of stones with little lanterns and a secret
yard. This house is your house. It cannot
be foreclosed. Close your mouth and take
out the dirty money. Give it away freely.
All the while, the river dances by
too fast for any real reflection.

# Morning

In cities across the world, men are turning
on lamps as women twist in the dream
of the car underground. The road-signs
say *Steep, Continue with Caution,* but the car
wants to calculate loss, to scoff at progress,
both tender and loyal. To lean back and roll.
Up ahead—white headlights—the dog-god
eyes of the insomniac regarding the petty
sleeper, her mouth wet and clenched like the
grip on a wheel. Body wrapped like one who
is falling, yellow highway ribbons a cursive
for breath, heartbeats; tiny soldier staking
his claim. They lie like this in one bed.
Sheets, cotton and clean, clock clicking its
insistent pulse. Amazing, the distance
we live from one another, the dark that
we travel, unloading our suitcases of
small animal desire. Alone as one must
be to navigate those lower roads until
morning, when she hands him the cup.

# Notes

"The Paraclete" refers to Abelard and Heloise, 16th-century, ill-fated lovers. It is the name of the convent where Heloise retreated after her separation from Abelard.

In "Fish", "Before the bed, before the knife" are lines from Sylvia Plath's *The Eye-Mote*.

"Pomegranates Turn Upward", "Stichomancy" and "Everything" are made up almost entirely of fragments of found language from *The New Yorker* magazine.

## Acknowledgements

I would like to thank the following institutions, teachers, friends, partners and exes who helped make these poems, and this book, possible: The Corporation of Yaddo, The Fine Arts Work Center in Provincetown, Blue Mountain Center, The New York Times Fellowship, New York University, The Poet's House, Aimee Gallin, Alfred McDonnell, Amanda Jones, Amani King, Amy Rathgeb, Andrew Altschul, Ann Lauterbach, Anne Haven McDonnell, Ariel Friedman, Art Corriveau, Art Estin, Ashlie Kauffman, Carla Roitz, Carley Moore, Carol Tierney, Caroline Crumpacker, Cathy James, Christina Malfitano, Coles Burroughs, Craig Carpenter, Daphne Taylor, David Petersen, Eileen Myles, Elizabeth Koster. Elizabeth Scarboro, Elizabeth Sullivan, Elizabeth Worz, Elline Lipkin, Emily Cass McDonnell, Eve Pearlman, Fiona Neary, Forest Melchior, Gabriel Metcalf, Galway Kinnell, Gil Cass, Gina Magid, Gretchen Elkins, Holly McClelland, Idra Novey, James Huang, Janice Fitzpatrick-Simmons, Jean Valentine, Jennifer Firestone, Jennifer Tseng, Jessie Lendennie, Jimbo Blachly, Jo Walsh, Joaquin-Baca-Asay, Jody Gold, Jody Madell, Joelle Hann, John Ashbery, Jon Loomis, Joseph Legaspi, Josh Kurtz, Juliana Spahr, Karyn Kloumann, Kathleen McDonnell, Kaya Hope Friedman, Kim Sproule-Wright, Larissa Szporluk, Laura Eastman, Laura Sims, Leah Souffrant, Lee-Ann Brown, Lisa Sperber, Lynn Melnick, Madeline Cass-Estin, Malinda Markham, Mari L'Esperance, Mark Woods, Martha Sharpe, Michael Allison, Prageeta Sharma, the Po-Moms, Rachel Levitsky, Rachel Swersey, Robert Kelly, Sarah Braunstein, Sharon Olds, Sinead Daly, Spring Ulmer, Stacey Rees, Stacy Leigh, Suzan Alparslan, Taeko Onishi, Tim Davis, Tim Earley, Tom Devaney, Tom Peters, Victor LaValle and William Matthews.

Ariel Friedman

## About the Author

Caitlin Grace McDonnell was a New York Times Fellow at NYU in 1995-97, where she was awarded the Washington Square Poetry Award. She has received fellowships from Yaddo, Blue Mountain Center and the Fine Arts Work Center in Provincetown. Currently, she teaches English in NYC public schools, and hangs out with her three-year-old daughter, Kaya Hope.

Made in the USA
Charleston, SC
27 March 2013